Acting
Animals

ABDO
Publishing Company

A Buddy Book by
Julie Murray

VISIT US AT
www.abdopublishing.com

Published by ABDO Publishing Company, 8000 West 78th Street, Edina, Minnesota 55439.

Printed in the United States.

Coordinating Series Editor: Rochelle Baltzer
Editor: Sarah Tieck
Contributing Editor: Marcia Zappa
Graphic Design: Maria Hosley
Cover Photograph: *iStockPhoto:* Abel Leão, Centrill; *Photos.com:* Jupiter Images.
Interior Photographs/Illustrations: *AP Photo:* AP Photo (p. 21), Jennifer Graylock (p. 19), Lennox McLendon (p. 25), Chris Park (p. 26), Douglas C. Pizac (p. 7), Chris Pizello (p. 20), Don Ryan (p. 17), David Zalubowski (p. 13); *Getty Images:* AFP (p. 15), Evan Agostini (p. 29), Frederick M. Brown (p. 23), CBS Photo Archive (pp. 10, 11, 18), Margaret Chute (p. 9), Marc Grimwade/WireImage (p. 27), Hulton Archive (p. 9), Kevin Winter/Image Direct (p. 30); *iStockPhoto:* Shanna Hendrickson (p. 5), Konstantin Kirillov (p. 29), Marcel Pelletier (p. 5), Rick Rhay (p. 7), Eliza Snow (p. 5); *Wikipedia.com* (p. 30).

Library of Congress Cataloging-in-Publication Data

Murray, Julie, 1969-
   Acting animals / Julie Murray.
      p. cm. -- (Going to work. Animal edition)
   ISBN 978-1-60453-560-0
   1. Animals in motion pictures--Juvenile literature. 2. Animals on television--Juvenile literature. I. Title.

PN1995.9.A5M87 2009
791.43'662--dc22

                                                              2008042426

Contents

Animals At Work

Going to work is an important part of life. At work, people use their skills to accomplish tasks and earn money.

Animals can have jobs, too. Many times, they complete tasks that human workers can't.

One job animals have is acting. They **perform** in live shows, on television, and in movies. Some even **pose** for **photographs**. People enjoy their work.

Many kinds of animals can be trained as actors.

In The Spotlight

Acting animals **perform** for the pleasure of **audiences**. There are many different types of work for acting animals.

A chimpanzee might appear in a movie. A tiger might perform in a live show at a zoo. And, a dog might be **photographed** for a magazine **advertisement**.

Acting animals must be comfortable with the many different people and animals they meet while working.

HISTORY LESSON

Animals have been acting for hundreds of years! Even before movies and television, they **performed** in live shows. These included circuses, magic shows, plays, and zoo shows.

Motion pictures were invented in the 1890s. Soon, animal actors began appearing in them.

In the 1930s and 1940s, more than one famous chimpanzee appeared in the *Tarzan* movies. Jiggs was the first. He died in 1938.

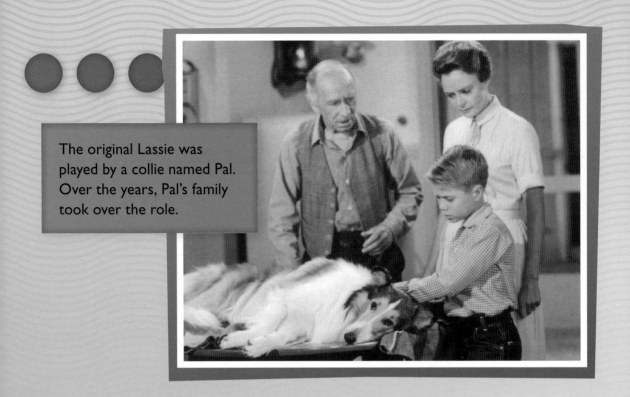

The original Lassie was played by a collie named Pal. Over the years, Pal's family took over the role.

Televisions were invented in the 1920s. By the 1950s, many families had televisions at home. Animal actors started to become famous on television.

Lassie was a popular television show in the 1950s and 1960s. It was about a heroic dog named Lassie.

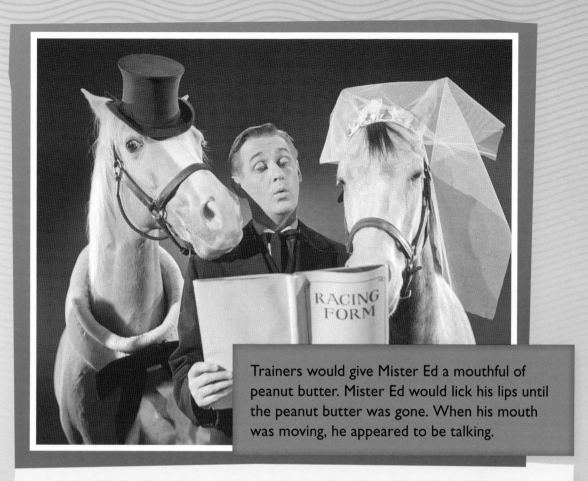

Trainers would give Mister Ed a mouthful of peanut butter. Mister Ed would lick his lips until the peanut butter was gone. When his mouth was moving, he appeared to be talking.

In the 1960s, the television show *Mister Ed* also featured an animal actor. A horse named Bamboo Harvester played a talking horse called Mister Ed. When he became famous, his name was changed to Mister Ed.

Working Together

Some acting animals are pets. Others are not. Some are hired for one **shoot**. Others travel and **perform** in shows.

It is important that acting animals enjoy performing. Many of them have natural talent. Trainers help them work better. They teach the animals commands and simple tricks. This can take years.

Capuchin monkeys are known for being smart and curious. They can live to be about 40 years old! Whiplash is more than 20 years old.

Did You Know?

Whiplash the Cowboy Monkey performs in live shows. He has also starred in Taco John's television advertisements.

Work Safety

Sometimes, acting animals are hurt while training or performing. This used to happen often. But today, people work to keep these animals safer.

Groups protect acting animals. They make sure people treat the animals well. They also make sure animals are safe on sets.

Today, people create images of acting animals on computers. Then, the computer animals do unsafe or difficult work. In 1995, the movie *Babe* used both a real and an animated pig.

On The Set

Animals that appear in television shows and movies are often paid as actors. Many **perform** tricks or use special skills.

When animals have starring **roles**, the story centers on their characters. Animals with starring roles have a lot of work to do! They are an important part of the movie or television show.

In 1993, an orca whale named Keiko starred in *Free Willy*. The movie was about a friendship between a boy and a whale. Throughout his life, Keiko continued working with trainers on his performing skills.

Animals work with trainers to prepare for their **roles**. Trainers teach the animals to follow directions during filming. Also, they care for the animals on the **set**.

Mister Ed learned many different skills for his role on *Mister Ed*.

In 2007, Leo and Ginger played Underdog and "Sweet" Polly Purebred in the movie *Underdog*.

On the **set**, acting animals see and hear many things that are different from their regular lives. So, they practice with trainers until they can **perform** in different surroundings.

Manly plays Sharpay's dog in the *High School Musical* movies. He is director Kenny Ortega's pet.

Sometimes animals appear alongside stars in television shows or movies. Though they may only be in a few scenes, they serve important roles.

Every animal that appears in a television show or a movie must behave properly. It must follow instructions and commands when the camera is filming.

In the 1940s and 1950s, a horse named Trigger became famous. He appeared with cowboy Roy Rogers on television and in movies. Even though Rogers was the star, Trigger had many fans.

Strike A Pose

Some acting animals **pose** for **photographs**. Posing for photographs is called modeling. These pictures are often used for **advertisements**.

Almost any type of animal can model. Snakes, spiders, rabbits, and dogs all model. Animal models must be **groomed** and well behaved. Many animals are paid to be models!

Over the years, several cats have posed as Morris the Cat. Morris appears in advertisements for 9Lives Cat Food.

In 1968, animal trainer Bob Martwick found the first cat to play Morris at an animal shelter. In 2006, 9Lives Cat Food began to help homeless cats like Morris. It found homes for 1 million cats!

Did You Know?

Live Shows

For more than 100 years, acting animals have appeared in live shows. They do tricks for circuses and magic shows. Some also act in stage plays.

Live shows are often exciting. But, working with animals in front of a live **audience** can be unsafe. Sometimes animals become scared or behave in unexpected ways.

Siegfried & Roy was a famous show in Las Vegas, Nevada. It combined magic with tiger acts. In 2003, Roy Horn (*above*) was attacked and badly hurt by a tiger during a live show. The show was closed after the attack.

SeaWorld is a theme park in Florida, Texas, and California. It hosts live shows featuring whales, dolphins, and other sea creatures.

People can also watch animals **perform** live at zoos and amusement parks. There, they can see the animals up close. They also learn about the animals at special shows.

The Australia Zoo is located in Queensland, Australia. Crocodiles and other animals appear in live shows there.

Gifted Workers

Acting animals do **challenging** tasks. They often show the bond between humans and animals. Many people connect with the animals they see **perform**. Acting animals do meaningful work that brings people enjoyment.

Acting animals have special skills and talents that amaze people!

Many animal actors are treated like celebrities. Gidget, who starred in Taco Bell advertisements, has attended movie openings!

29

The Animal Times

Changing Lives

More than 80 percent of dogs and cats in movies come from animal shelters. People adopt homeless pets from these shelters.

Me Cheeta

One former *Tarzan* actor, Cheeta, was 76 in 2008. He was recognized as one of the oldest-living chimps!

Me Cheeta is a book about Cheeta's life and work. It came out in October 2008.

Important Words

advertisement (ad-vuhr-TEYZE-muhnt) a short message in print or on television or radio that helps sell a product.

audience (AW-dee-uhns) a group of people that listens to or watches a show.

challenging (CHA-luhn-jihng) testing one's strength or abilities.

groom to make neat and tidy in appearance.

perform to do something that requires skill in front of an audience.

photograph (FOH-tuh-graf) a picture made with a camera.

pose to hold a special position while one's picture is made.

role a part an actor plays in a show.

set the place where a movie or a television show is recorded.

shoot the action of taking a picture or filming a movie with a camera.

Web Sites

To learn more about acting animals, visit ABDO Publishing Company online. Web sites about acting animals are featured on our Book Links page. These links are routinely monitored and updated to provide the most current information available.

www.abdopublishing.com

Index